FIVE BIKES

A collection of poems paying tribute to the heroic children in our group homes, foster homes and social service programs--hearing their heartache, sharing their hopes

Jean B. McGee

Copyright © 2007, 2020 Jean B. McGee

All rights reserved

The characters and events portrayed in this book are fictitious. Any similarity to real persons, living or dead, is coincidental and not intended by the author.

No part of this book may be reproduced, or stored in a retrieval system, or transmitted in any form or by any means, electronic, mechanical, photocopying, recording, or otherwise, without express written permission of the publisher.

ISBN-13: 9798678847751

Cover design by: Art Painter
Library of Congress Control Number: 2018675309
Printed in the United States of America

CONTENTS

Title Page	1
Copyright	2
Introduction	7
Dedication	9
FIVE BIKES	11
THE POWER OF CARDS	12
TO LANGSTON HUGHES	13
HEARTBROKEN	14
TO STUDENTS WHO CAN'T READ	15
WAITING	16
CONFUSION	17
FROM MISSISSIPPI AND KATRINA	18
POWER OF PERSPECTIVE	19
INCORRIGIBLE	20
MISFIT	21
A WAY OF LIFE	22
COLLAGES	23
CHAOS TO ORDER	24
"CAN I SIT IN YOUR LAP?"	25
CHANGE	26
GRAY SUITCASE	27

ONCE THE VICTIM, ALWAYS THE VICTIM.	28
NINTH GRADE	29
WEDNESDAY	30
AFFIRMATION	31
WRITE SENTENCES?	32
MIXED UP KID	33
SELF ESTEEM	34
HAIR TO-DO?	35
SOME ARE HARD TO PLACE THEY SAY	36
FROM THAT TO THIS	37
HAPPY BIRTHDAY	38
HIS POEMS	39
MANIPULATION	40
GUIDANCE?	41
WHAT IS GOING ON?	42
SCARRED	43
LEFT BEHIND	44
SUCCESS	45
BURNT	46
AWRY	47
THE HEAVINESS OF EMPTINESS	48
CHOICE	49
TRUTH	50
MAYBE	51
IDENTITY	52
LITTLE DO WE KNOW	53
PERMANENT RECORD	54
LYRICS	55

| YOU NEVER KNOW | 56 |
| About the Author | 57 |

INTRODUCTION

The last 24 years of my teaching career I was blessed to be in the position to work with group home residents throughout Greenville County on a one-to-one basis. They were in grades one to twelve and all were multi-disadvantaged yet had the pluck to keep going, keep learning and to hope for a better life. Hopefully these poems will increase awareness that these students are enrolled in our schools and living in our communities across the country. The opportunities to touch their lives are immense: send a card; pat a back; tutor one to one; be interested and listen, have conversations; look at the tangible evidence of their lives, find their interest and reading level and take an appropriate book; encourage positive choices, be a mentor. They don't need another bike; they need human caring and involvement on a one-to-one level.

DEDICATION

For all group home residents, especially Nathan.

These poems are tributes to all the group home residents I've worked with through the years. They persevere and struggle against all odds. While most of us look to family and home for stability and support, most of these students have been abused and neglected by theirs. They are moved from place to place like pawns on a game board. Many have physical, emotional, and/or mental handicaps. Many have learning disabilities. They all are multi-disadvantaged yet they are blessed with loads of pluck. They each and every one amaze and inspire me. They have been my life tutors.

FIVE BIKES

He flashes his big white smile
on his dark little face,
his bright eyes deceiving
as he sees letters, numbers
as some indecipherable code.

He's packed again
as he's moving again
to another foster home.

As we sit and chat, saying our good-byes,
his teacher walks by
and says cheerily through the door,
"We're giving you a new bike
to take with you."

He turns to me with a sudden sad face
and says softly,
"Now I have five bikes."

THE POWER OF CARDS

How is it cards can say

YOU EXIST?

My students save them, treasure them,
carry them around
as if without them they would disappear.

Usually they're from acquaintances,
strangers, anyone nice enough to send a card.

I met a wheelchair-bound man once
who kept lists of boys' birthdays
residing at group homes
and sent them cards,

What a powerful simple gift.

Last night,
one of my ex students came for a visit.
He went back out to his car to get his cards
then showed me the ones I'd sent through the years
along with all the others.

It's scary the memories we are making
and not making.

TO LANGSTON HUGHES

I carry your poems, books, bookmarks
from group home to group home
from school to school
from year to year

and scatter your words
like beads of hope
to faces that light up as they hear this music
they can feel and soon can read.

I hand out copies of your poems
like someone on a street corner
trying to save souls.
We read and reread
which is a miracle for the many young black boys
that cannot read or barely read or hate to read.
We talk of dreams and holding them tight
and steps to make those dreams come true.

Almost a hundred years later,
this southern white teacher
and a black poet from Harlem
team up and bring moments of hope.

HEARTBROKEN

This middle school boy
has never lived away from home before

and now is placed in a group home

filled

with tough middle and high school boys.

He crawls into his trunk,
so he can hide and cry.

He pulls the heavy wardrobe from the wall
and squeezes behind it,

so he can hide and cry.

TO STUDENTS WHO CAN'T READ

He's over six feet tall
with long blond wavy hair swept back
wearing a tight sleeveless black T shirt
and long silver chain, looking so cool.

He has a seat, and we talk
about home, school, interests
before starting the reading test.
He mumbles, now slouching in his chair,
"I hate reading."
(which means I can't read)

And he can't, and my heart breaks.
I treat them so gently,
these students who reveal this wound to me.

WAITING

Every Friday afternoon he waits -----
his clothes packed,
he sits by the window and watches
for someone in his family to come,
to take him home for the weekend.
They tell him they're coming each week.

He believes them each week.
But they never come.

CONFUSION

I attempt to administer achievement test
as this thirteen year old sniffles and talks
obsessively about it all:

How he wants to go home
How he does not want to go home
How he hates this group home
How he wants to stay

How he misses the arguing, the fighting,
all the comfortable pain of home.

FROM MISSISSIPPI AND KATRINA

New student from emergency shelter
Comes into my room
And talks and talks

(I postpone the testing)

Of fear
Of bodies in trees
Of coffins floating by
Of water everywhere

The familiar and the unfamiliar
Her life upside down

And
Her mother arrested on drug charges
In the middle of it all
Leaving her daughter in the custody of DSS.

So here she is
At a new high school
Far away from home
Trying to be cute, okay
At fifteen.

POWER OF PERSPECTIVE

He waddles into my room
with his curly hair, pleasant face,
chubby body,
always chubbier
lost in jackets and stuff
overflowing from pockets, bookbag
as if somehow more secure lost in it all.

Coming from art class
his chubby hands hold a lumpy
misshapen clay mask
of blues browns
that looks like a battered bruised boy.

"It's ugly! I hate it!
I'm throwing it in the trash!"

"Let's see James. Oh, I like it. In fact,
it's just what I need. Look!
It's a perfect pencil holder."

I place pens, pencils into eyes, nose, mouth.
His scowl relaxes a little into a smile.
His life suddenly useful, nice.

INCORRIGIBLE

The teacher warns me
about this incorrigible kid
who is nothing but trouble.
"Send him back to class if a problem."

He tells me through a usual headache
of being shot three times in LA
a brother dead of a gunshot at 18
a glass table broken over his head
and on and on and then

Of loving to read, write poems, draw
Of wanting to be an architect.

We read Langston Hughes' "Dreams."

MISFIT

She is huge, tall and large,
and would have been out of place
in middle school or high school.
Yet here she is in elementary school
with ribbons in her hair
and trying to fit
into this tiny chair in the library!

A WAY OF LIFE

This special education student
is emotionally handicapped?
And who wouldn't be?

He's been in foster care all his life.
He has had twenty eight placements
in his sixteen years, and how many schools,
how many teachers, how many
beginnings and endings?

I'm amazed that he's here
and smiling and coping at all.

And again, he's packed, ready to move.

COLLAGES

She pulls from her bookbag
large framed collage of pictures of her son
and shows and shares
telling of the road that brought her here.
So now in the ninth grade
with a year old child
and a whole life ahead,
she's worried about her baby
as he is in another foster home
while other teens worry about their hair.

CHAOS TO ORDER

On this rainy, dreary morning
Tommy, usually shy and reserved
despite his teenage history
meets me at the door.
He holds a jigsaw puzzle
that I had given him the previous week.
Now completed on a large board
in his proud hands,
he beams
showing me the chaos of his life
turned
into flowers, sailboats, blue skies.

"CAN I SIT IN YOUR LAP?"

Twinkly blue eyes and charming innocent smile
turn up to me from this four year old waif
and he asks, as I'm opening a book
to read to another child,
"Can I sit in your lap?"

Where is your Mama? Where is your Daddy? Where
are your grandparents, aunts, uncles, cousins?
Where is your church, your community? Where is
someone with a lap? DSS does not have a lap.
It doesn't seem a lot to ask.

"Of course you can.
Come on, let's read a book."

CHANGE

His mama's in jail.
His daddy's in jail.
His brother's in jail.
His uncles and cousins are in jail.

This student's life shaped
in the mold of drugs and crime
and we expect him to act right and to achieve
which he has never known.

He is seeing a new possible life
from living at stable group home
and some high school successes
but the old life tugs fiercely at his heels
like a mad dog pulling him back.

GRAY SUITCASE

Little fellow though fifteen
lugs his gray suitcase upstairs
into my room with him for tutoring
and everywhere else that he goes.
It is with him at all times
as surely as the glasses on his face.

He opens and shares the contents
telling the story of each item
gathered over his years of moving:
a small radio with no batteries, two yo yos,
a cheap camera with no batteries or film,
Jedi cards, two thin rocks,
a Chicago Bulls baseball cap,
and a small notebook.

And this is it
Except for a few clothes in his room.

ONCE THE VICTIM, ALWAYS THE VICTIM.

(this despairing line was told to me by a director of a group home as I was expressing my concern over these young people being treated as objects)

This little figure reminds me of an old man
instead of a second grade boy
he seems so unusually battered.
And yes he was born into a family
that had battered, abused, neglected.

He brings a list of spelling words
from his classroom teacher
to learn to spell and make sentences:
family, mother, father, brother, sister.

And the pain continues.
Must he say the words, make sentences,
spell them over and over
while the other boys and girls
make lovely sentences?

NINTH GRADE

Over the years,
he has been my student several times
while living at different group homes
so he's glad to see me
at his new high school
because I know his secret
and I will help him read his schedule
so he can find his classes.

He loves conversation
and talking about his family
and his weekends at home.
so I write his stories,
and I read his stories back to him,
then he reads his stories back to me.
And he talks more
and he wants me to write more
so he can read more.

WEDNESDAY

Small high school boy lugs in his stuff,
his large glasses sliding down his nose,
and settles into chair beside me.
he intently digs through his book bag
and says, "Look what I brought to show you!"
as twelve year old yellow
National Geographic Magazines emerge.
"I brought them for $5.00," he says.
"Do you carry them around every day, all day?"
I ask.
"No, just today, Wednesday, to show you."

We flip through issue after issue
as if scanning a candy counter
trying to pick one article to read.
He picks a long article
on archaeological digs in Peru
with glorious pictures of tombs and mummies.

Together we read, taking turns
as we discuss, examine, imagine,
working on reading skills, unnoticed.

AFFIRMATION

One of my students
walks into my office at the high school
with his hand full of cards
and tells me scheduled student is absent
so could he stay instead?

His birthday had been a few days earlier
and he wants to show me his cards.
One by one,
he explains each word, each design,
each stamp, every detail of his nine cards.
He tells me in his soft voice
the little he knows of each sender
as he slips each affirmation
back into its cover
and leaves with his hand full of proof.

WRITE SENTENCES?

He's overweight
wears very thick glasses
and a baseball cap
pulled tight on his head
as he wanders from library
to healthroom, to special ed class
to my room as if he can't sit still.
He has a speech impediment
and illegible handwriting
due to severe
motor coordination handicap
yet his teacher sends a note weekly
"Get him to write sentences."
Even though he can barely hold a pencil??
We read and discuss and he learns.

MIXED UP KID

"I'm just a mixed up kid. I need help. I wish I was like other kids and had a mama. I have all this anger inside me. Will you listen to me every time I come?"

"Yes. I will."

SELF ESTEEM

Another new student comes into my room for testing. He enters telling me all about himself in a confident but nervous manner.

"I am ADD and I have muscular dystrophy and I cannot read or do math but my Mama has been fixed so that she will not have any more children like me."

HAIR TO-DO?

Pale, timid fourteen year old boy
speaks softly as we talk—
his face peeping from huge amount of
long, bushy, red curly hair.

He loves hard rock and plays bass he says
and also loves to skateboard with his friends.

Surprising me,
he comes eagerly for tutoring each week
and is responsive and wants to do more,
to learn more math.

His little sister was placed in another group home
and he wants to be moved there to be with her
though he knows nothing about the place.

But after an interview,
they won't admit him unless he cuts his hair,
the one thing he can control
in his chaotic life
and the one thing
that gives him some identity.

Today, I'm at his group home
and he's leaving this week
and joining his little sister
since, yes,
he sat in the barber chair and cried
as his hair was cut.

SOME ARE HARD TO PLACE THEY SAY

He's over six feet tall
and has a fuzzy mustache,
but he cannot read
and computes math at a fourth grade level
though in high school.

Today, he has a small red floppy teddy bear
hanging over his shoulder
and tells me that the bear keeps him company.
His other constant companion and solace
is his thumb.

He's been at the emergency shelter
for months over his 90 days;
some are hard to place they say.

FROM THAT TO THIS

I check on beautiful, bright
high school student who always comes
for her tutoring session
but not today.

She says that she skipped classes
because her head hurts
from chunks of hair being pulled out
in a fierce fight at the group home,
that she is scratched and bruised
and miserable.

She looks a wreck,
this week matching her inner and outer worlds.
Her dad's in jail, her grandmother unfit;
nowhere to live;
too many absences to earn credits.

And so from that to this.

HAPPY BIRTHDAY

Handsome young man looking sad and troubled
tells me that it is his birthday.
He's sixteen and in the seventh grade!

He's been tending his sick mother
in a remote trailer for years
with no phone, no car, little money.

He says she's very obese and a chain smoker
just admitted to the hospital
for triple by-pass surgery,
and he was placed in this group home.

Immediately the trailer burned
with all their meager possessions gone
including the loss of his little pet dog.

We complete the test
and confirm that he is a bright young man.
We talk of possibilities and goals and hopes
of happy birthdays ahead.

HIS POEMS

At first he was withdrawn, reluctant
but this handsome, muscular black boy
who wanted to become a boxer
became an eager student
after we read about Ali and other black heroes
and Langston Hughes' poems.

His face lit up; he wanted copies;
he started a folder of poems
and read and reread them and asked for more.
This tough high school boy was in DJJ* custody
but he loved these tender hopeful poems
and would say with a glow, "That's beautiful."

One Monday,
they tell me that he is gone,
that he was taken in handcuffs
back to a detention center.

I hope he managed to pack his poems.

*Department of Juvenile Justice

MANIPULATION

This ninth grader has a project
assigned on Costa Rica

And she cannot read at all
but it's no problem.

She says with a shrug
that she can do it all on the internet:

Find pictures, copy an article
cut and paste and turn it in.

She'll make an A and not learn one thing.

GUIDANCE?

He'll soon be twenty
and only has 18 credits
of the 24 that he needs to graduate.
And he cannot pass the math exit exam
after taking it numerous times.
Yet he stays in high school hoping
he will somehow get a diploma.

And all he wanted was to take culinary arts
at the vocational center and be a cook?

WHAT IS GOING ON?

He sits in the library
with his special education science book
and four sheets of chapter tests
and tries to fill in the blanks and match

even though he was out of school the last week
and did not hear the discussion
about faults and mantles and crusts.

But he tries hard and wants to do well
so they move him into mainstream classes
even though he cannot read
even though he doesn't know
how many months are in the year
but he's sitting now
in English I, Algebra I, World History.

SCARRED

Another beautiful bright girl
comes for tutoring
often smiling and pleasing
but also erupting like a volcano
onto anyone, anytime, anyplace.

She ran away from her abusive home at fourteen
and lived on the streets,
using drugs and stripping for money.
Her young arms now dotted with scars.
Her young mind and soul dotted with scars.

LEFT BEHIND

He'll soon be seventeen
in the ninth grade
and here near the end of school
he has all Fs for the year
and no wonder
as he reads at fourth grade level
and computes math at fifth grade level.

Yet here in high school
he's studying Romeo and Juliet
and studying inequalities in Algebra
and listening to classical music in the halls
so everything would be all right.

SUCCESS

He now holds college degrees,
Rents his own apartment,
Loves his community,
Is successfully employed,
And still determined, moving forward.

Yet he struggles always
with his past
with his meaning
with his pain—

always the effort to rise above,
to surface into new life.

BURNT

He has huge burn scars on his large dark arms
and he seems to be burnt within
as he is so withered in spirit.

He cannot read though in high school
so I pull out Langston Hughes's book of poems
and I share
some of the simple, rhythmic ones with him.

He lights up, he wants copies, he practices.

I wish you could hear him read
"My People" and "Dreams"
in his soft confident voice.

AWRY

They tell me
that she poured bleach
onto the others' clothes
and even poured bleach into their tea
so she's taken away to girls' juvenile prison.

I tutored
a kind girl, a polite girl,
a good student
who had plans for her life
now gone horribly awry.

THE HEAVINESS OF EMPTINESS

She's unkempt, quiet, sullen,
always sleepy and depressed
existing behind very thick walls,
heavy walls where no one can reach.
She seems erased.
Empty.

Yet somehow, and this is the miracle:
she manages to plod
through the halls
from class to class
through minutes all soaked
in the heaviness of emptiness.

CHOICE

I go to second grade classroom to get student new to the school as just placed in an emergency shelter nearby.

The teacher is quite relieved to have him leave for an hour as she tells me that he is disruptive, loud, ill mannered and on and on.

He immediately tells me that he hates everything and everybody.

He would not talk anymore, nor read, nor count, nor listen to me read as he would put his fingers in his ears.

So I read softly to myself as he watched with his fingers in his ears.

The next week at his classroom door, he asks, "Do I HAVE to go?"

I answer that no he does not have to go, that I have other boys and girls that want to come for extra help and I would love it if he would but maybe he would like to think about it for a week?

He immediately wants to come and is a most eager student remembering his folder, memorizing poems, choosing to learn.

TRUTH

Pretty, confused, verbal, heartbroken,
but finally sure
as she shakes, sobs, talks.

She ran away from home that was hell
and tells truth
of drinking, drugging,
hitting, lying, even raping
and of younger brother hanging himself

and of three helpless little sisters there
and now her parents hating her, threatening her
for leaving and telling the truth.

And this is family! This is home!

MAYBE

He's trying his best to be good and do good
and stay out of trouble
because he has some dreams.

His mama tends his disabled dad
and three younger brothers
in a rented trailer far out in the country.
His twenty year old sister
lives next door in a rented trailer
expecting her fourth child any day.

He's trying
to hold fast to his dreams.
Maybe.

IDENTITY

He seems determined to have a difficult life
as all the family patterning
has settled in as normal
and he is following along
without a thought.

He hates school,
comes for tutoring with no book, no pencil,
no paper, no plan.
He successfully stays in trouble
at his school,
at his group home
as if in constant need of punishment.

We talk about other goals, hopes and dreams
but they are so distant for him
that he cannot see.

He's back in juvenile prison.

LITTLE DO WE KNOW

Looking like all the other teens
busy in the new high school library
she tries to read, make notes on Robert Frost
as she tells me of her first night
in the emergency shelter:

She couldn't sleep,
her dad was killing her for telling.
Over and over the same nightmare,
she even heard the sound of his truck
crunching on the gravel driveway.
Finally her bed wet with sweat,
she got up and wrote and wrote in her journal
trying to be rid of the demons
her dad shoved into her.

He was probably sleeping fine
across town out on bail.

PERMANENT RECORD

So many manila folders are rubber banded
into his unwieldly permanent record
containing so many schools, foster homes,
group homes, tests, placements,
that he cannot remember his own life.

Yet
he wants to learn, to finish his work,
so we can talk.
He wallows in wonderful conversations
about anything and everything.

He's eager to build things,
to be a carpenter
to nail order from disorder.

LYRICS

Tall high school boy saunters sadly
through life and into my room,
cap atop his head,
cords dangling from earphones
hooked to radio in his pocket.

So each session
he puts it all away
and attempts to do his math.
One day amidst the math and light conversation
I ask him about his music
and discover that he loves lyrics
and writing his own lyrics
and writing poems as I do.

So we finish the math in record time
and scramble for our folders
as our eyes twinkle and our voices lift
in the new shared place of learning.

YOU NEVER KNOW

The others laugh at his odd looks, dress, ways
and strange language that he speaks.
One day he tells me how to cure my cough,
"Git some white liquor and mix it with honey
And lemon, like my grandma done."

But he loves words, poems,
and trying to "get his feelings down"
so I give him a paperback dictionary
which he carries with him all the time,
staff tells me
and reads it like a novel.

A week later it is worn.

ABOUT THE AUTHOR

Jean McGee is a retired teacher who lives near Greenville, SC. For 24 years she served as Title 1 tutor for group home residents throughout Greenville County. She attended Furman University and Clemson University for her BA and MED degrees. Her best times are those with her large wonderful family. Her favorite hobbies are reading and gardening.

Mauldin, SC
jbmcgeefinally@aol.com

Made in the USA
Monee, IL
12 January 2021